The Startup's Guide to Non-Disclosure Agreements

Tennille Christensen and Mariam Amin

Tech Law Garden, Copyright 2017

Table of Contents

PREFACE 1

CHAPTER 1: PARTIES 3

CHAPTER 2: PURPOSE 8

CHAPTER 3: LIMITATIONS 12

CHAPTER 4: RESIDUALS 22

CHAPTER 5: CHOICE OF LAW 26

CHAPTER 6: VENUE 28

CHAPTER 7: DEFINITION OF CONFIDENTIAL INFORMATION 30

CHAPTER 8: EXCEPTIONS TO CONFIDENTIAL INFORMATION 36

CHAPTER 9: AS IS; WARRANTY DISCLAIMER 48

CHAPTER 10: REMEDIES 51

CHAPTER 11: LIMITATION OF LIABILITY 56

CHAPTER 12: TERM AND TERMINATION OF NDA 61

FINAL THOUGHTS: 67

Preface:

This book is designed to introduce startup employees to important concepts in non-disclosure agreements (NDAs), also known as confidentiality agreements (CA), confidential disclosure agreements (CDA), proprietary information agreements (PIA), or secrecy agreements (SA).

A common question in the startup or small business context is "Should I have an attorney review this contract?" It is always best to have an attorney review every contract including NDAs, since they are binding agreements that the company will have to honor. However, many business executives end up skimming and signing NDAs without any legal input due to time constraints, lack of access to a qualified attorney, lack of financial resources, or a misperception that they aren't "real" contracts that could harm the company. The goal of this short guide is simply to highlight many of the big picture issues that attorneys consider when reviewing NDAs. This information is meant to be a general education on the topic of NDAs, not legal advice, and does <u>not</u> and could not cover all of the potential issues that may arise in connection with NDAs.

Chapter 1: PARTIES

The first thing you need to know about any contract is who the parties are. A "Party" is a person or entity involved in an agreement.[1] A party can enter into a contractual transaction, file a lawsuit, and defend its rights. There are several questions to ask when trying to understand who the parties to a contract are:

- What type of entity is each signatory (Individual? Corporation? LLC?)?

- Is it in good standing?

- Where is each signatory located?

- Any history of bad press or red flags that come up when you research the identities of the party?

- Who will you be dealing with (who is the actual signer?) and are they able to bind the legal entity?

---

[1] *The People's Law Dictionary.* (2005). Retrieved June 27 2014 from http://legal-dictionary.thefreedictionary.com/party

Why do the parties matter? First, if a startup operates as an LLC or a C corporation, it needs to enter all contracts as the legal entity and not as the individuals who sign the agreements. This is for two reasons:

1) To preserve the corporate liability shield and protect the individuals signing;

2) To ensure that the <u>company</u> as a whole is bound to the contract, not just the signing individual.

Similarly, the specific identity of the parties is important. If you believe you are working with only one company, but in reality, you will be disclosing information to them and all of their sister and brother companies within a larger group of companies controlled by a parent, this may change your opinion about how much you wish to disclose what uses of the information should be allowed.

Others associated with the Party:

The NDA may refer to others who are associated with the Party. These third parties can include affiliates, subcontractors, advisors, permitted receivers, and others as defined in the agreement.

- **Affiliates:** An Affiliate is usually a person, entity, subordinate, member, organization, or subsidiary party that either has control over the party in the contract or is controlled by the party in contract. Affiliates typically have common owners or directors, shared business interests, or control of one another through ownership. A common example of an Affiliate is a foreign subsidiary or parent entity.

- **Subcontractors:** A subcontractor, (or "contractor") is one who contracts with a primary contractor to perform some or all of the primary contractor's obligations under a contractual agreement. A common example of a subcontractor is a hosting services provider that a company uses to host an online software service.

- **Advisors**: An advisor is a person who gives official or professional advice, typically as an expert in a particular field. Advisors can be legal, financial, technical, and general. A common example of an advisor in the startup context is a previously successful entrepreneur who is mentoring the current leadership of the startup.

- **Permitted Receivers:** A Permitted Receiver is someone explicitly identified in the NDA as being permitted to receive or have access to the Confidential Information governed by the NDA.

Permitted Receivers identified in the NDA become linked to the actual party identified in the NDA and will have access and the ability to use information as set forth in the agreement.

In summary, knowing the details of the opposing party is the first step to understanding issues or concerns that could arise from your disclosure of information to them, or receipt of Confidential Information from them under an NDA.

Chapter 2: PURPOSE

A _purpose_ is an objective or end to be attained.[2] The purpose for which the parties share their information is central to understanding and evaluating an NDA. In order to know what the appropriate use limitations and distribution permissions are that should be included in the document, you first need to understand the purpose of the parties for entering into discussions. Like many terms, the term "Purpose" may have a slightly different meaning in the legal context than in the day-to-day context.

The legal purpose is the reason why the parties are entering into the NDA. It should be defined within the NDA and should limit each party's rights and responsibilities with respect to the other party's Confidential Information.

---

[2] _Merriam-Webster._ (2014). Retrieved June 30, 2014 from http://www.merriam-webster.com/dictionary/purpose

Sales or Service Partnerships

Suppose you are evaluating whether your company (Party should enter into a partnership with Party B, to co-sell your products into the same customer channels, or to determine if you may be able to work together to jointly market complimentary products and services. To make this evaluation, both parties will need access to some of the other party's Confidential Information.

In this case, a proper description of the purpose in the NDA would be *"to survey or evaluate the other party's product and services to understand the feasibility of a mutual marketing arrangement."* In contrast, *"to develop new products based on the other party's information"* or *"to incorporate information into a party's product offerings"* would <u>not</u> be appropriate purposes of the agreement because neither party intends to authorize the other party to do those things in this scenario.

Potential sales and mergers

Another common NDA use case is a potential business sale, merger, or acquisition. In these types of transactions, the purpose of the NDAs is different, for example *"evaluating a potential acquisition of the other party's business."* Both parties have an interest in limiting discussions and ensuring that their Confidential Information and trade secrets are not used or disclosed by the other party for any purpose other than deciding whether to enter the proposed transaction or sale.

Broad catch-all purpose

Often, parties enter into NDAs under a broad catch-all business purpose such as: *"The purpose of evaluating/entering a mutually agreeable business transaction between the parties."* This broad description is useful when you may not know where the discussions may lead. This purpose allows flexibility while ensuring that the information is not used for anything that doesn't benefit both parties. The key protection here, if applied correctly, is that everything permitted by the agreement has to be mutually agreeable to both parties.

Some best practices to keep in mind:

1) If you know the specifics of the intended use of the disclosed information, then limit the purpose language to cover only that particular transaction or use.

2) If you do not know where discussions are heading, then make the purpose of the NDA broader, and make sure to include the term "mutually agreeable" or some other similar protections in the purpose language.

Chapter 3: LIMITATIONS

The following limitations are usually present in most NDAs:

(1) Standard of Care.
(2) Use Prohibition.
(3) No copying.
(4) No Distribution.
(5) No license granted.

These limitations may not be clearly laid out for you in this particular order, although some may be clustered together, as discussed below. If you don't recognize the presence of limitations that you need, you may want to request additional language to cover them. Ask yourself if there are particular ways the other party could use your information that you would want to prohibit? There are innumerable special cases and unique limitations that can arise in NDAs, but the five limitations listed above are the most common.

(1) Standard of Care

Standard of Care is a legal duty of care owed from one party to another based on surrounding circumstances. By signing an NDA with an explicit standard of care, the receiving party agrees to treat (store, handle, use) the discloser's Confidential Information in accordance with the stated standard.

A commonly used standard of care is to require the other party to treat your information in the same manner the party treats its own Confidential Information. Other common standards of care are to require that the other party treat your Confidential Information in a manner that is *"commercially reasonable" or in "strict confidence."*

Example:
> *"The Receiving Party agrees to use at least the same degree of care (but no less than a reasonable degree of care) that the Receiving Party uses with respect to its own similar information to prevent unauthorized disclosure or use of such Confidential*

Information."

A secondary issue to consider with respect to the standard of care is whether the Party is responsible for the failures of its third party recipients.

This issue only arises when a party is not contractually prohibited from distributing or sharing your information with third parties (for example, Subcontractors, Affiliates, Advisors, and Permitted Receivers, as defined in Chapter 1).

Depending on the NDA language, your Confidential Information could be shared by the recipient with a third party that has no legal relationship or actual responsibility to you. In that case, you may need to require language in the NDA that creates liability for the other party in the event of the third party's breach of confidentiality.

If you are going to allow the other party to distribute

your information to third parties with whom you do not have a contractual relationship, then you need the other party to commit to (i) ensure that the standard of care is contractually extended from it to its third parties or (ii) be responsible for any breach of that standard of care by such third parties.

Examples:

1. *"The Receiving Party may disclose Proprietary Information to its employees, agents, and representatives who have a need to know such information for the purposes set forth in this Agreement, provided that all such employees, agents, and representatives must be bound by contractual obligations at least as protective of the Disclosing Party in this Agreement. The Receiving Party shall be responsible for any breach of this Agreement by such employees, agents, and representatives."*

2. *"The Recipient is responsible for any acts or omissions of its Representatives that, if taken by the Recipient, would constitute a breach of this Agreement."*

(2) Use

A use limitation defines the allowed uses of the Confidential Information. Use limitations are usually in the beginning of NDAs near the stated purpose (and often are directly tied to the purpose), but there is no hard and fast rule. Without a proper use limitation, the receiving party may use your information for any purpose, including purposes you did not intend, for example to build a product that competes with yours or to offer similarly competitive business terms to customers.

Examples:
1. *"Without limiting the generality of the foregoing, the Receiving Party will only use or reproduce the Disclosing Party's Confidential Information to the*

extent necessary to enable the Receiving Party to fulfill the purposes contemplated by this Agreement."

2. Recipient agrees to use Discloser's Confidential Information for the sole purpose of evaluation in connection with the Project and discussions with Discloser related to the Project, or as otherwise agreed upon in writing by an authorized representative of Discloser."

3. "Recipient will not use Discloser's Confidential Information for any purpose except in connection with exploring a potential transaction."

4. "The Recipient may use the Confidential Information solely for the purpose of evaluating Discloser's potential use of Company's products and services (The Purpose)."

5. "Receiving Party shall not otherwise use, or permit

any others to use, any Confidential Information for any purpose other than the Purpose described in Section II, without the prior written consent of the Disclosing Party."

(3) No Copying

If a party has access to your Confidential Information, you may or may not want them to be authorized to make copies of it. Look for the language in the NDA that discusses copying and confirm that it correctly protects your information and only allows copies to the extent you wish to permit them.

Examples:
1. *"Recipient <u>will not copy</u>, distribute, or otherwise use the Information or knowingly allow anyone else to do the same, provided that Recipient <u>may copy</u>, internally distribute, and use the Information <u>solely in pursuit of the Project</u>."*

2. "Recipient agrees <u>not to copy, duplicate, disclose or deliver all or any portion of the Confidential Information</u> to any third party."

(4) <u>No Distribution</u>

If a party has access to your Confidential Information, you may or may not want them to be authorized to distribute it or copies of it. Read the NDA and ensure you understand the permitted distributions, if any. Also review all distribution limitations and confirm that they correctly protect your information and only allow distribution to receivers that you want to have access to your information.

Example:

"Recipient shall not copy, <u>distribute</u>, or otherwise use such Information <u>or knowingly allow anyone else to</u> copy, <u>distribute</u>, or otherwise use such Information."

(5) No license

If a party has access to your Confidential Information, and that information is also subject to protection under intellectual property rights, it is best to make it explicitly clear that no license to any intellectual property is being granted under the NDA. An NDA is <u>not</u> the proper document to be granting IP rights. To avoid the risk of unexpectedly doing so, it is best to be clear that no IP rights are being conveyed.

Examples:

1. *"<u>No license</u> under <u>any intellectual property right is granted</u> under this Agreement or by any disclosure of Confidential Information except as expressly stated in this Agreement."*

2. *"Nothing contained herein shall be construed, <u>either expressly or implicitly, to grant to the Receiving Party any rights to technology or a license</u> under any patent, copyright, trademark or other intellectual property*

right now or hereafter in existence except for the limited Purpose set forth herein."

3. "The parties recognize and agree that <u>nothing contained in this Agreement shall be construed as granting any property rights, by license or otherwise,</u> to any Confidential Information of the other party disclosed pursuant to this Agreement, or to any invention or any patent, copyright, trademark, <u>or other intellectual property right</u> that has issued or that may issue, based on such Confidential Information."

Chapter 4: RESIDUALS

A residuals clause is a tricky carve-out to the NDA's protections. Typically, a residuals clause exists to ensure that the free unaided memories of a receiver or its employees aren't restricted. The goal of a good residuals clause is to avoid trouble at some point in the future if the receiver of Confidential Information relies upon unaided memory for a different activity (that may be outside of the purpose of the NDA).

A residuals clause typically contains two parts: 1) a definition of residuals and 2) broad permission to use the residuals. Residuals clauses can cause problems if the "secret sauce" being disclosed under an NDA is possible to memorize or otherwise falls under the definition of residuals.

Examples:
1. *"Notwithstanding anything herein to the contrary,*

either party may use Residuals (as defined below) for any purpose or in any manner. The term 'Residuals' means any information retained in the unaided memories of a party's Representatives who have had access to the other party's Confidential Information pursuant to the terms of this Agreement. A person's memory is unaided if the person no longer has access to the Confidential Information and has not intentionally memorized the Confidential Information for the purpose of retaining and subsequently using or disclosing it. <u>Neither party has any obligation to limit or restrict the assignment of such persons or to pay royalties for any work resulting from the use of Residuals.</u>

2. "The term 'residuals' shall mean Information in intangible form, such as ideas, concepts, techniques and knowhow, which may be retained in the mind of those employees who have had rightful access to the

Information. *Each party shall be free to use the residuals of the Information for any purpose,* subject to the patent, copyright and trademark rights of the Discloser."

3. *"Receiver shall be free, at any time, to use the Residual Information retained by those of its employees* who have had access to the tangible form of the Materials or Confidential Information received from Licensor, for any purpose, including the use of such Residual Information in the development, manufacture, marketing and maintenance of Receiver's products and services. 'Residual Information' shall mean that information in non-tangible form (subject only to the patent, copyright, and maskwork rights of Licensor and the obligation not to disclose such information during the period of confidentiality) which may be retained by Receiver's employees who have had access to the Materials or

Confidential Information."

Each of the underlined provisions above highlights the manner in which the residuals are carved out from the protections of the NDA and made available for uses outside of the purpose.

Chapter 5: CHOICE OF LAW

A choice of law provision is a clause that sets forth which state or country's law will govern the NDA. Every sovereign state has its own governing body of law for the interpretation of contractual agreements. As such, it is important to understand the differences between default choice of law and contractual choice of law provisions.

If choice of law is absent, the NDA will be governed by the default choice of law, which could default to a number of places: where the agreement was signed, where one party operates a business, where a party is incorporated, or where the transactions or uses contemplated by the NDA take place.

For example, an agreement signed and executed by two parties who operate in the same state is most likely to default to the laws of that state. If, however, the parties operate their businesses in different states or multiple states, then there could be a conflict over which state's laws should apply. An express choice of law contractual provision eliminates these ambiguities.

An explicit contractual choice of law is enforceable against both parties. The body of law that determines which law applies is called "conflict of laws." It is very common to see contractual choice of law provisions expressly disclaim conflicts of laws provisions of the selected state to avoid any unexpected consequences.

Example:
"This Agreement shall be subject to and governed by the laws of the state of California without regard to its provisions regarding conflict of laws."

Chapter 6: VENUE

Venue is the geographic location where a legal cause of action (such as a complaint filing, hearing, or other dispute resolution process) takes place. A venue clause determines which specific court or alternative dispute resolution body is the proper location for a plaintiff to bring an action. There are two types of venue that can govern an NDA: (1) default and (2) contractual. In the absence of a venue clause, default venue laws apply, and a party may be sued wherever the opposing party can assert legal action.

A venue clause that is expressly written in the agreement results in a contractual agreement that all disputes relating to the contract will be resolved in the identified venue. Many companies prefer to limit venue to local courts or alternative dispute resolution bodies to avoid travel in the event of a dispute.

Examples:

1. "Any an all disputes between the parties relating to this Agreement will be resolved in the state and federal courts located in San Francisco, California, to whose jurisdiction the parties hereby irrevocably submit."

2. "Any dispute, claim or controversy arising out of or relating to this Agreement or the breach, termination, enforcement, interpretation or validity thereof, including the determination of the scope or applicability of this agreement to arbitrate, shall be determined by arbitration in San Francisco, California before one arbitrator. The arbitration shall be administered by JAMS pursuant to its Comprehensive Arbitration Rules and Procedures."

Chapter 7: DEFINITION OF CONFIDENTIAL INFORMATION

The definition of Confidential Information is set forth in NDAs to clarify what is and what is not protected. Confidential Information can be contractually defined as a general category of information received (e.g. all information that a reasonable person would consider confidential in nature) or it can be drafted as a list of specific items (e.g. presentations, data, financial analysis, and charts). Each and every NDA should expressly define the Confidential Information it governs—be sure to review the definition and confirm that you understand and agree about the information (both yours and the other party's) that will be governed by the NDA.

Examples:

1. *"'Confidential Information'* <u>*means any and all information and material disclosed by one party (the 'Disclosing Party') to the other party (the 'Receiving*</u>

Party') during the term of this Agreement that is marked as (or provided under circumstances reasonably indicating it is) confidential or proprietary, or if disclosed orally or in other intangible form or in any form that is not so marked, that is identified as confidential at the time of disclosure. Confidential Information includes the Purpose, discussions concerning the Purpose and timing or location thereof."

2. *"Each undersigned party (the 'Receiving Party') understands that the other party (the 'Disclosing Party') has disclosed or may disclose information relating to the Disclosing Party's business (including, without limitation, ideas, inventions and other technical, business, financial, customer and product development plans, forecasts, strategies and information), which to the extent previously, presently or subsequently disclosed to the Receiving*

Party is hereinafter referred to as 'Proprietary Information of the Disclosing Party."

Some definitions further define Confidential Information as only information that is marked and/or summarized. Marking and summary requirements act to ensure that only what is clearly marked or identified as "confidential" or "proprietary" will be protected under the NDA. These types of provisions are often followed by a deadline to send a summary of oral disclosures in writing (e.g. 5, 15, 30 days after disclosure). If you fail to send a summary by the deadline, then the Confidential Information you disclosed orally and did not summarize will <u>not</u> be protected by the NDA.

Marking and Summary Examples:
1. *"A recipient of Confidential Information under this Agreement ('Recipient') shall <u>have a duty to protect only that Confidential Information which is</u>*

(a) disclosed by the Discloser in writing and is marked as confidential at the time of disclosure, or which is (b) disclosed by the Discloser in any other manner and is identified as confidential at the time of the disclosure and is also summarized and designated as confidential in a written memorandum delivered to the Recipient's representative named above within 30 days of the disclosure."

2. *"Notwithstanding the foregoing, nothing will be considered 'Confidential Information' of the Disclosing Party unless (A) the Disclosing Party provides the Receiving Party with a non-confidential written summary of the matter to be disclosed prior to disclosure only after the Receiving Party has consented in writing and (B) (1) it is first disclosed in tangible form and is conspicuously marked 'Confidential' or the like or*

(2) it is <u>first disclosed in non-tangible form and orally identified as confidential at the time of disclosure and is summarized</u> and delivered in tangible form <u>conspicuously marked 'Confidential' or the like within 30 days of the original disclosure</u>."

3. **(Optional marking and summary)**

   "<u>Although there is no marking requirement,</u> Confidential Information, provided in written, encoded, graphic, or other tangible form shall be deemed to be confidential and proprietary if it is clearly marked 'confidential.' If the Confidential Information is provided orally, it shall be deemed to be confidential and proprietary if it is so identified by the Disclosing Party at the time of such disclosure or if by its nature it should be deemed confidential. Within five (5) days of making oral confidential statements, the

Disclosing Party may confirm that such statements were confidential and proprietary by submitting a written description of said Confidential Information to the Receiving Party. Confidential Information shall include such information disclosed thirty (30) days prior to the Effective Date of this Agreement and which relates to the Purpose."

"'Confidential Information' shall mean any information, including but not limited to data, techniques, protocols or results ... which is reasonably necessary for the Purpose, and which (i) <u>if disclosed in tangible form, is marked as 'Confidential' at the time it is disclosed</u>, or (ii) if disclosed in non-tangible form (including without limitation orally or visually), <u>is identified as confidential at the time of disclosure and is summarized by Company with specificity in a writing marked 'Confidential' and given to the</u>

other party within thirty (30) days after such disclosure."

Chapter 8: EXCEPTIONS TO CONFIDENTIAL INFORMATION

Exceptions to Confidential Information are often found after the language defining it. Before executing an NDA, it is important to understand what exceptions to Confidential Information exist, and whether you can accept that the information that falls under those exceptions will not be protected. As a receiver of another's Confidential Information, there are five common exceptions that you may want in the NDA:

(1) In the public domain; publicly known.
(2) Previously known to the recipient.
(3) Disclosed to the recipient by a third party (without breach of a confidentiality obligation).
(4) Independently developed.
(5) Disclosed under operation of law (but solely to the extent of that disclosure)

.

(1) In the public domain; publicly known

If something is in the public domain or is generally known, the receiving party will want that information to be excluded from the definition of what is covered as Confidential Information. The reason for this is simple—If someone shares something with you that is commonly known, they shouldn't be able to limit how you can use the information. Without the NDA, you would have been able to discover it and use it freely.

Examples:

1. *"Confidential Information shall not include information that (a) <u>is or becomes publicly available</u> through no act or omission by the Recipient."*

2. *"The information <u>becomes publicly available</u> other than by the Recipient disclosing it in violation of this Agreement."*

3. *"Notwithstanding the foregoing, the confidentiality and non-use obligations of the Receiving Party under this Agreement shall not apply to Confidential Information which <u>is within the public domain at the time of disclosure or that subsequently enters the public domain</u>."*

4. *"Without granting any right or license, the Disclosing Party agrees that the foregoing shall not apply with respect to any information after five years following the disclosure thereof or any information that the Receiving Party can document <u>is or becomes (through no improper action or inaction by the Receiving Party or any affiliate, agent, consultant or employee of the Receiving Party) generally available to the public</u>."*

5. *"Confidential Information will not include, or will cease to include, as applicable, information or materials that (i) <u>were generally known to the public</u> on the Effective Date; (ii) <u>become generally known to the public</u> after the Effective Date, <u>other than as a result of the act or omission of the Receiving Party</u>."*

(2) Previously known to the recipient

If the recipient previously knows the information before it is disclosed to them, the recipient will want to continue to be able to use the information despite the disclosure under the NDA. This explains why the "previously known" exception typically exists in NDAs.

Examples:

1. *"Recipient <u>already has or knows the information</u> at the time provided by*

Discloser"

2. "Confidential Information shall not include information that ... (b) <u>was already in Recipient's possession</u> without restriction before receipt from the Disclosing Party and was not subject to a duty of confidentiality;"

3. "Confidential Information will not include ... information or materials that <u>were rightfully known to the Receiving Party prior to its receipt thereof from the Disclosing Party</u>."

4. "Disclosing Party agrees that the foregoing shall not apply with respect to any information ... that the Receiving Party can document <u>was in its possession or known by it without restriction prior to receipt from the Disclosing Party</u>."

(3) Disclosed to the recipient by a third party without breach of a confidentiality obligation

Similarly, if information is properly disclosed to the recipient by a third party (without breach of confidentiality), the recipient will want to be able to use the information in whatever manner the third party allows, regardless of whether it was also disclosed by the disclosing party under the NDA.

Examples:

1. *"Confidential Information shall not include information that ... is rightfully disclosed to Recipient by a third party without confidentiality restrictions."*

2. *"Confidentiality and non-use obligations of the Receiving Party under this Agreement shall not apply to Confidential Information which ... is lawfully received from a third party free to disclose such Confidential*

Information to the Receiving Party."

3. *"Disclosing Party agrees that the foregoing shall not apply with respect to any information after five years following the disclosure thereof or any information that the Receiving Party can document was rightfully disclosed to it by a third party, provided the Receiving Party complies with restrictions imposed thereon by third parties."*

(4) Independently Developed

Independent development is likely the most contentious of these five exceptions. On one hand, a receiver of information may wish to be free to develop similar information or inventions. On the other hand, a discloser of information may be concerned that the receiver will take their information and use it to develop competing technology or business and simply claim that they independently developed the information.

This tension is often resolved by specifying in the NDA what <u>exactly</u> constitutes independent development. A party can propose to qualify the independent development using limiting language, such as "without use of the Confidential Information" or "by recipient's employees without access to the Confidential Information." The goal is to limit "independent" development in a manner that preserves protection for the receiver but also allows the discloser to feel comfortable that their information won't be misused.

Examples:
1. *"The Recipient <u>independently develops the same information without use of the Discloser's Confidential Information</u>."*

2. *"Notwithstanding the foregoing, the*

confidentiality and non-use obligations of the Receiving Party under this Agreement shall not apply to Confidential Information which: ... b) <u>is independently developed by the Receiving Party, without reference to, use of or access to the Confidential Information</u>."

3. "Disclosing Party agrees that the foregoing shall not apply with respect to any information after five years following the disclosure thereof or any information that the Receiving Party can document <u>was independently developed without use of or reference to any Proprietary Information of the Disclosing Party</u>."

4. "This Agreement imposes no obligation upon the Recipient with respect to

Confidential Information which is independently developed by the Recipient by employees without access to the Confidential Information."

(5) Disclosed under operation of law

The last common exception to the definition of Confidential Information confirms that a recipient is allowed to legally comply with a government request should one arise. Disclosers of Confidential Information may wish to limit this exception by requiring the recipient to follow certain procedures, such as seeking a protective order or requiring that the exception only applies to the single instance of the required disclosure under operation of law (e.g. that all other disclosures and uses in violation of the NDA are still prohibited).

Examples:
1. *"The Receiving Party may make disclosures*

<u>required by law or court order provided the Receiving Party uses diligent reasonable efforts to limit disclosure and to obtain confidential treatment or a protective order</u> and allows the Disclosing Party to participate in the proceeding."

2. "The Recipient may disclose the Disclosing Party's Confidential Information <u>as required by law or court order provided: (i) The Recipient reasonably notifies the Disclosing Party in writing of the requirement for disclosure unless notice is prohibited by law;</u> and (ii) discloses only that portion of the Confidential Information as is legally required."

3. "This Agreement imposes no obligation upon the Recipient with respect to

Confidential Information which...<u>is disclosed under operation of law or court order provided the Recipient Party uses diligent reasonable efforts</u> to limit disclosure and to obtain confidential treatment or a protective order and allows the Disclosing Party to participate in the proceeding."

Chapter 9: AS IS; WARRANTY DISCLAIMER

The first thing to note regarding an "AS IS" provision or "WARRANTY DISCLAIMER" is that you will not always see one in an NDA. Typically, the party disclosing information under the NDA would want to include this disclaimer if they have any concerns that use of the information they are disclosing could result in unexpected or harmful results.

The "AS IS" provision is shorthand for a longer, more specific warranty disclaimer. When one disclaims a warranty, he or she is removing the specific quality assurances that may ordinarily come with the product or service (or in the case of an NDA, information) being provided.

A warranty is a type of legal protection that comes along with whatever is being provided to another party. In NDAs, some people like to be very clear that the

Confidential Information they are providing is provided "AS IS" without any representation or assurance of quality. In other words, if you rely upon this information and you are harmed, it's not the disclosing party's fault. Another common way to think of an "AS IS" disclaimer is *caveat emptor* or BUYER BEWARE. In the case of NDAs, the item being "bought" (exchanged) is the Confidential Information.

Examples:

1. *"ALL CONFIDENTIAL INFORMATION IS PROVIDED 'AS IS.' NEITHER PARTY MAKES ANY WARRANTIES, EXPRESS, IMPLIED, OR OTHERWISE, REGARDING THE CONFIDENTIAL INFORMATION, INCLUDING WITHOUT LIMITATION, ANY WARRANTIES OF MERCHANTABILITY, FITNESS FOR A PARTICULAR PURPOSE OR NON-INFRINGEMENT."*

2. "The Discloser warrants that it has the right to disclose the information provided to the Recipient. Otherwise, the information is provided 'AS IS' and without any warranty."

3. "Disclosing Party shall have no liability whatsoever for any damages arising out of Receiving Party's use of Confidential Information disclosed pursuant to the Agreement, and all Confidential Information disclosed by the Disclosing Party hereunder shall be on an 'AS IS' basis and with no warranties of any kind, express or implied."

Chapter 10: REMEDIES

There are a few remedies available for breach of an NDA:
*Damages.
*Injunctions and Temporary Restraining Orders (TROs).
*Specific Performance.

(1) Award of Damages

An award of damages is the most common and traditional remedy under civil law. Damages are an award of monetary value in the event of a breach of agreement where the goal is to provide the harmed party with the financial amount required to make up the harm caused by the breach. Proving the value of the loss that results from an NDA breach is difficult. It is very hard to point to information disclosure and show a direct financial or property harm that results. Even if you can show a direct financial harm, the actual loss is extremely difficult to quantify if the information has become generally known, and thus the loss will continue in the future. Accordingly, some NDAs contain provisions indicating that monetary damages are likely to be insufficient.

Example:

> "*Notwithstanding the above, the parties agree that in certain circumstances of breach of obligations under this Agreement, monetary damages may not be adequate and that the non-breaching party shall be entitled to apply to a court for injunctive relief in addition to any other available remedies, and the party alleged to have breached this Agreement shall not oppose any such application in the matter of damage.*"

(2) Equitable Relief: Injunctions, Specific Performance

Injunctions

Injunctions (including temporary restraining orders) are equitable remedies where a court orders an entity to take an action or stop taking action(s). In the case of an

NDA, the ordered action would be to prevent or stop a breach such as the sharing or use of Confidential Information in violation of the NDA.

Examples:
1. *"Accordingly, <u>the Parties specifically agree that the Disclosing Party shall be entitled to seek injunctive or other equitable relief to prevent or curtail any such breach</u>, threatened or actual, without posting a bond or security and without prejudice to such other rights as may be available under this Agreement or under applicable law."*

2. *"The unauthorized use or disclosure of Confidential Information by the Recipient could cause the Discloser irreparable harm, for which the Recipient could not adequately compensate the Discloser after the fact. <u>Because of this, the parties agree</u>*

that if the Discloser believes the Recipient has breached (or might breach) this Agreement, the Discloser may seek an injunction to stop the unauthorized use or disclosure. Just because the Discloser has the right to seek an injunction does not mean it gives up its other rights—the Discloser may still assert other rights and remedies available to it."

Specific Performance

Specific Performance, a judicial order requiring the actual performance of the specific obligations (and conditions, if relevant) bargained for in the contract, may be awarded by the court in exceptional circumstances where monetary damages are not an adequate remedy and there is danger of substantial harm to the wronged party. In the case of NDAs, a breach of an obligation not to use trade secrets to compete with the owner of the trade secrets, for example, would be a good candidate for seeking specific performance if the discloser could show likelihood of serious harm.

Specific performance is a rarely awarded remedy, and in the case of NDAs, an injunction is the much more likely non-damages remedy that will be sought by an aggrieved part. But, it is theoretically possible that specific performance of the obligations of the NDA could be sought in parallel with an injunction against further use or dissemination of the Confidential Information.

Chapter 11: LIMITATION OF LIABILITY

A limitation of liability is an agreement between the parties to limit the possible losses or damages that may arise in connection with agreement. These clauses specifically list and limit the different types of damages that may arise. Damages fall into two distinct categories: Indirect Damages and Direct Damages. Limitation of liability provisions may also put a cap on all possible monetary recovery under the contract, which if reasonably drafted, could be upheld. Liability may be a set dollar amount or be generally limited, for example, limiting damages to the aggregate amount paid or payable under the contract in the twelve months prior to when the claim arose.

Direct Damages

Direct damages are the damages that directly result from a breach of contract. A full disclaimer of direct damages means that there is no expectation of recovery if the contract is not performed, and therefore, the contract would be unenforceable. It is quite common in many contracts, however, to limit the total monetary value of direct damages to the amounts expected to be paid, expended, or received under the contract.

Direct damages are sometimes referred to as *Expectation Damages*—that is, what you would have received from the other party if the contract had been fully performed as you expected. In the case of an NDA, the disclosing party's expectation is that the receiving party will not disclose or misuse the Confidential Information. Accordingly, an award of direct damages is difficult to quantify in terms of money for breach of an NDA.

Indirect Damages

Indirect damages are consequential, indirect, or

associated damages arising from the breach of contract, meaning they are not the expected outcome of performance of the contract, but rather they are losses that arose as a result of the breach of the contract. Indirect damages also include incidental and special damages.

In commercial contracts, it is very common to limit or exclude indirect damages entirely for many types of breach. However, in the case of NDAs, it is important to remember that your only financial losses resulting from a breach of the NDA are likely to be indirect losses, such as lost profits, lost business opportunities (due to someone using your information to compete with you), lost market share (due to additional competitors), etc. If you are the disclosing party, it is generally not a good idea to enter into an NDA (or other obligation of confidentiality) where indirect damages are disclaimed entirely, as you will have difficulty showing any other damages.

An example of a typical commercial indirect damages disclaimer NOT recommended for an NDA follows:

> "NEITHER PARTY WILL BE LIABLE TO THE OTHER OR ANY THIRD PARTY FOR <u>CONSEQUENTIAL, INCIDENTAL, INDIRECT AND/OR SPECIAL DAMAGES</u> FOR ANY CLAIMS ARISING FROM OR IN ANY WAY CONNECTED WITH THIS AGREEMENT, EVEN IF THE POSSIBILITY OF SUCH DAMAGES IS, OR SHOULD HAVE BEEN, KNOWN."

If there is a disclaimer of indirect damages, it's best to address the need for damages resulting from breaches of confidentiality by expressly carving out Confidential Information and intellectual property losses from any disclaimer of indirect damages (whether in an NDA or commercial contract):

Example:

"EXCEPT FOR BREACH OF CONFIDENTIALITY OBLIGATIONS UNDER THIS AGREEMENT OR BREACH OF THE OTHER PARTY'S INTELLECTUAL PROPERTY RIGHTS, BOTH OF WHICH SHALL BE UNLIMITED, IN NO EVENT WILL EITHER PARTY BE LIABLE TO THE OTHER, FOR ANY INDIRECT, INCIDENTAL, EXEMPLARY, PUNITIVE, SPECIAL OR CONSEQUENTIAL DAMAGES OR LOSSES, INCLUDING WITHOUT LIMITATION, LOSS OF USE, PROFITS, GOODWILL OR SAVINGS, OR LOSS OF DATA, DATA FILES OR PROGRAMS, ARISING OUT OF OR IN CONNECTION WITH THIS AGREEMENT."

Chapter 12: TERM AND TERMINATION OF NDA

NDAs have two separate periods of time that matter: (1) a disclosure period and (2) a protection period. Generally speaking, the term of an NDA, is the disclosure period, or time period during which, disclosures of Confidential Information are deemed protected. The protection period, however, is how long these disclosures must be protected after they are made and often survives the NDA.

(1) NDA Disclosure Period

A disclosure period is the time when Confidential Information disclosed is covered by the NDA. An NDA will be valid until it reaches a certain expiration date or is otherwise terminated by the requirements set out in the agreement. If the NDA is silent as to the explicit term, it will be governed by the applicable state laws' default provisions regarding term and termination. Under some state laws, for example, when a contract is silent as to term, the default is that the agreement is terminable by either party for convenience upon notice.

Examples:
1. "*This Agreement applies only to disclosures made by the Parties to each other during the term of this Agreement, which shall end immediately upon written notice by one party to the other party of its intention to terminate this Agreement.*"

2. "*This Agreement shall terminate on the fifth anniversary of the last disclosure of Confidential Information by the Disclosing Party to the Receiving Party, but the Receiving Party's obligation to protect Confidential Information shall survive termination of this Agreement and shall continue in effect with respect to*

Confidential Information of the Disclosing Party that by its nature (for example, a trade secret) should reasonably be maintained as confidential after termination of this Agreement."

3. "<u>Unless extended by a mutually agreed written amendment, this Agreement shall terminate three (3) years after the Effective Date. Either Party may terminate this Agreement at any time without cause upon written notice to the other Parties.</u>"

(2) NDA Protection Period

A protection period is the period of time Confidential Information is protected under the NDA. The obligation to protect information begins after the receipt of Confidential Information and continues until the protection period expires, which is often purposefully drafted to be a period longer than the disclosure period (or term of the NDA). If an NDA is silent as to the protection period, then arguably, the obligations with respect to Confidential Information are only valid so long as the NDA is in effect (e.g. if the NDA is terminated, the obligation to protect the information goes away).

Examples:
1. "*Notwithstanding the earlier termination of this Agreement, the Receiving Party's obligations under this Agreement shall continue for a period of five years from the date of final disclosure.*"

2. "*This Agreement shall terminate on the fifth anniversary of the last disclosure of Confidential Information by the Disclosing Party to the Receiving Party, but the Receiving Party's obligation to protect Confidential Information shall survive*

termination of this Agreement and shall continue in effect with respect to Confidential Information of the Disclosing Party that by its nature (for example, a trade secret) should reasonably be maintained as confidential after termination of this Agreement."

3. *"Receiving Party's obligations with respect to Confidential Information disclosed hereunder during the Term will survive any termination of this Agreement."*

Destruction of Information

Often, in connection with termination of an NDA, the receiving party will have an obligation to destroy (or return) the Confidential Information it received. This provision provides additional assurances for the disclosing party that its Confidential Information is less likely to be misused after termination.

Example:

"Upon termination of this Agreement or written request by a Disclosing Party, the Receiving Party shall: (i) immediately cease using the Confidential Information, (ii) <u>return or destroy the Confidential Information and all copies</u> (except copies required for backup, disaster recovery, or business continuity and in such case the obligations hereunder shall survive until such copies are destroyed), notes or extracts thereof to a Disclosing Party within fifteen (15) business days of receipt of request, and (iii) upon request of a Disclosing Party, confirm in writing that a Receiving Party has complied with these obligations."

Final Thoughts

We hope we've resolved some of the mystery behind the language in NDAs and made you more confident in reading and understanding them. As always, there is no substitute for legal review by your attorney, but in the event you are unable to obtain legal review, we hope this publication is useful. Although this publication does not constitute legal advice and its authors are not your attorneys, we certainly would love any feedback you may have and welcome your questions or comments.

www.ingramcontent.com/pod-product-compliance
Lightning Source LLC
Chambersburg PA
CBHW040838180526
45159CB00001B/235